25.50

SCIENCE STARTERS

Temperature

by Carolyn Bernhardt

BLASTOFF! READERS
3

BELLWETHER MEDIA • MINNEAPOLIS, MN

Note to Librarians, Teachers, and Parents:

Blastoff! Readers are carefully developed by literacy experts and combine standards-based content with developmentally appropriate text.

Level 1 provides the most support through repetition of high-frequency words, light text, predictable sentence patterns, and strong visual support.

Level 2 offers early readers a bit more challenge through varied simple sentences, increased text load, and less repetition of high-frequency words.

Level 3 advances early-fluent readers toward fluency through increased text and concept load, less reliance on visuals, longer sentences, and more literary language.

Level 4 builds reading stamina by providing more text per page, increased use of punctuation, greater variation in sentence patterns, and increasingly challenging vocabulary.

Level 5 encourages children to move from "learning to read" to "reading to learn" by providing even more text, varied writing styles, and less familiar topics.

Whichever book is right for your reader, Blastoff! Readers are the perfect books to build confidence and encourage a love of reading that will last a lifetime!

This edition first published in 2019 by Bellwether Media, Inc.

No part of this publication may be reproduced in whole or in part without written permission of the publisher. For information regarding permission, write to Bellwether Media, Inc., Attention: Permissions Department, 6012 Blue Circle Drive, Minnetonka, MN 55343.

Library of Congress Cataloging-in-Publication Data

Names: Bernhardt, Carolyn, author.
Title: Temperature / by Carolyn Bernhardt.
Description: Minneapolis, MN : Bellwether Media, Inc., 2019. | Series: Blastoff! Readers. Science Starters | Includes bibliographical references and index. | Audience: 5-8. | Audience: K to 3.
Identifiers: LCCN 2017061617 (print) | LCCN 2018009251 (ebook) | ISBN 9781681035451 (ebook) | ISBN 9781626178120 (hardcover ; alk. paper) | ISBN 9781618914682 (pbk. ; alk. paper)
Subjects: LCSH: Temperature–Juvenile literature. | Temperature measurements–Juvenile literature.
Classification: LCC QC271.4 (ebook) | LCC QC271.4 .B47 2019 (print) | DDC 536/.5-dc23
LC record available at https://lccn.loc.gov/2017061617

Editor: Christina Leaf   Designer: Josh Brink

Printed in the United States of America, North Mankato, MN

Table of Contents

A Day at the Beach

You feel the hot sand between your toes. The sun shines on your shoulders. It is a beautiful day at the beach!

4

You walk into the waves and feel cool water splash you. This is temperature at work!

What Is Temperature?

Temperature is how hot or cold something is. We cannot see temperature, but we feel it.

Temperature is measured
in units called **degrees**.

degrees

Measuring Temperature

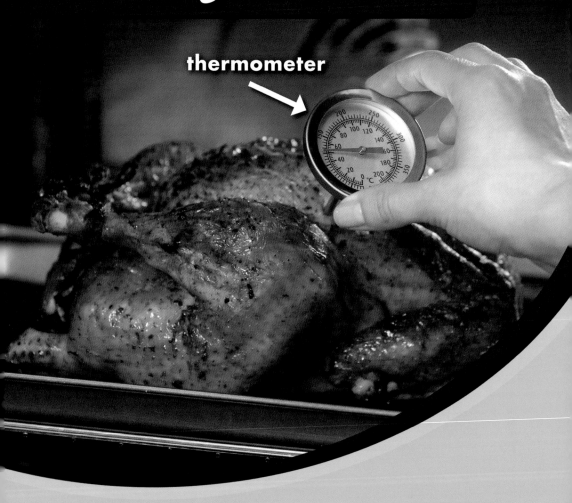

thermometer

You can measure temperature with a **thermometer**. Several **scales** measure temperature. The main ones are **Celsius** and **Fahrenheit**.

In the United States, Fahrenheit is common. Most other countries use Celsius.

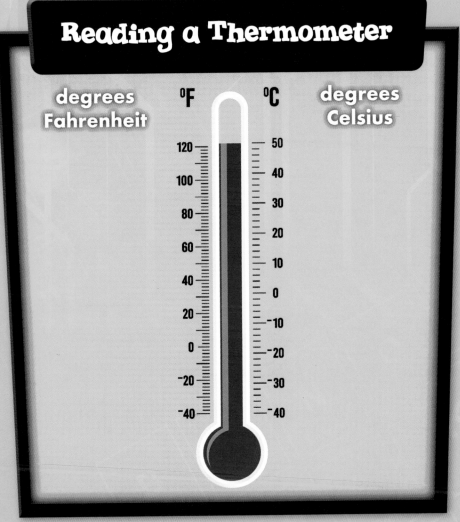

Reading a Thermometer

degrees Fahrenheit

°F

°C

degrees Celsius

Changing States

Temperature can change how something looks and acts. This is called changing states.

States of Matter

gas　　liquid　　solid

close-up look

There are three states of **matter**.
Solids keep their shape and size.
Liquids flow but keep their size.
Gases flow and continue to
spread out.

When a solid object reaches a high enough temperature, it **melts**. This means it turns into a liquid. If the temperature drops enough, the liquid **freezes** back into a solid.

melting ice

gas

When a liquid reaches a high enough temperature, it turns into a gas.

Most substances change states at different temperatures. Ice melts at 32 degrees Fahrenheit (0 degrees Celsius). Swiss cheese starts to melt at 150 degrees Fahrenheit (65.6 degrees Celsius)!

Melting Points

You can watch how different materials react to temperature in your own microwave! Have an adult help you with this activity.

What you will need:

- 1/4 cup chocolate chips
- 2 ice cubes
- 2 small cups (microwave safe)
- a microwave
- a thermometer
- a spoon to stir

---

1. Place the chocolate chips in one cup and the ice in the other.
2. Heat the chocolate in the microwave for 30 seconds, then stir. Repeat four times.
3. Carefully take the chocolate mixture out of the microwave and take its temperature with a thermometer. Record the temperature.
4. Clean off your thermometer while the melted chocolate is wet so it does not harden!
5. Heat the ice cube cup in the microwave for 2 minutes.
6. Carefully take the cup out of the microwave. Take the water's temperature with the thermometer. Which substance was hotter after 2 minutes in the microwave? What did you notice about the time it took for each substance to melt?

Body Temperature

Humans and many other animals, including cats and dogs, are **warm-blooded**. This means our bodies control their own temperature.

16

Human bodies are healthiest at 98.6 degrees Fahrenheit (37 degrees Celsius). If the body's temperature is much different, we can get sick.

Our bodies have several
ways to control temperature.

They keep cool with sweat when we get too hot. They keep warm by shivering when we are cold.

We can help control our bodies' temperatures, too. Shorts and light clothing in summer let heat escape easily from our bodies.

Coats and blankets keep heat in on cold winter days. Bundle up!

Glossary

Celsius—a scale for measuring temperature on which the boiling point of water is 100 degrees and the freezing point of water is 0 degrees; most countries use the Celsius scale to measure temperature.

degrees—units for measuring temperature

Fahrenheit—a scale for measuring temperature on which the boiling point of water is 212 degrees and the freezing point is 32 degrees; the United States uses the Fahrenheit scale to measure temperature.

freezes—changes from a liquid to a solid, usually because of cold

gases—matter that does not keep the same size or shape

liquids—matter that flows freely but stays the same size

matter—material that forms objects and takes up space

melts—changes from a solid to a liquid, usually because of heat

scales—series of spaces marked off by lines, used to measure amounts

solids—matter that keeps the same size and shape

thermometer—an instrument used for measuring temperature

warm-blooded—able to keep up a balanced body temperature that is mostly independent from the surrounding environment

To Learn More

AT THE LIBRARY
Bailer, Darice. *Measuring Temperature*. Ann Arbor, Mich.: Cherry Lake Publishing, 2014.

Fields, Hannah. *Keeping Warm with Fur and Fat*. New York, N.Y.: PowerKids Press, 2018.

Gardner, Robert. *How Hot Is Hot?*. Berkeley Heights, N.J.: Enslow Elementary, 2015.

ON THE WEB
Learning more about temperature is as easy as 1, 2, 3.

1. Go to www.factsurfer.com.

2. Enter "temperature" into the search box.

3. Click the "Surf" button and you will see a list of related web sites.

With factsurfer.com, finding more information is just a click away.

Index

The images in this book are reproduced through the courtesy of: charobnica, front cover (periodic table); John Dakapu, front cover (circuit); Anita van den Broek, front cover (hero); Haye Kesteloo, pp. 4-5; Andrey Arkusha, p. 6; GLandStudio, p. 7; Africa Studio, p. 8; MicroOne, pp. 9, 11 (states of matter); Foxys Forest Manufacture, pp. 10-11; Vladimir Sotnichenko, p. 12; JasonDoiy, p. 13; George Dolgikh, p. 14; Tamara JM Peterson, p. 15; Viktoriia Vyshnevetska, p. 16; PR Image Factory, p. 17; wundervisuals, p. 18; jaclynwr, p. 19; Sergey Novikov, p. 20; Ami Parikh, p. 21; Tarzhanova, p. 24.